POSITIVE ATTITUDE: THE SECRET WEAPON

Dr. Ajay Desai

INDIA • SINGAPORE • MALAYSIA

ISBN 979-8-89777-423-4

Contents

Preface

Every writer's journey is shaped by the people and the experiences that inspire them, and mine is no different. At the heart of my story are my parents, Sri Balvantrai Desai and Smt. Manek Desai, whose love, wisdom, and unwavering support have been my guiding light. They instilled in me values that shaped my perspective and taught me the importance of having the right attitude in life.

I am also deeply grateful to my family, who have been my constant pillars of strength. My wife, Sushma, has been a devoted companion, offering encouragement and understanding through every twist and turn of this journey. My daughters, Shivani and Rajvi, are my greatest pride, whose love and belief in me fuels my passion to grow and achieve more every day. Their presence is my greatest source of joy and motivation.

A Lesson in Attitude

As I reflect on the many lessons life has to offer, one stands out vividly—an enduring truth about the power of attitude. It's a lesson I first encountered not in a textbook, but in a simple moment shared with my mother, a school teacher whose classroom wisdom often found its way into our home.

I remember her holding two apples—one bruised, one flawless—and showing me that, while they appeared different on the outside, they were equally fresh and sweet inside. That day, she gently reminded me that how we view the world and others depends entirely on our attitude. Through her words and actions, she taught me to look beyond imperfections, to find beauty in differences, and to approach life's challenges with resilience and gratitude.

This perspective has shaped my journey, reminding me that while we cannot always control circumstances, we can choose how we respond to them. This book draws from that foundational lesson—a tribute to the transformative power of a positive attitude. It is an invitation to embrace life with curiosity, kindness, and the courage to see the good, even in the bruised apples of our experiences.

A Divine Note of Gratitude

Lastly, I bow my head in gratitude to the Almighty, whose blessings have been a constant source of strength, guiding me through life's ups and downs. It is through His grace that I have had the courage to embrace challenges, the wisdom to learn from them, and the humility to share these lessons with the world.

Dr. Ajay Desai is having 5 World Records in his name registered in World Book, Limca, Asia, India & London Book of Records, for imparting highest 7000 plus Corporate Trainings & Trained more than 5 Lakhs CEO's & Executives in the world since 25years.

Thank you

Dr. Ajay Desai

CHAPTER 1

The Power of a Positive Attitude / Unlocking Success

Imagine life as a journey. You're cruising along, encountering bumps, detours, and the occasional breathtaking view. Now, what if I told you that the most important tool for navigating this journey isn't your fancy car, your destination, or even the weather—but your attitude?

That's right. Your attitude acts as the lens through which you see and experience the world. And the best part? You get to choose how clear, colorful, or foggy that lens is. A positive attitude can transform challenges into stepping stones, strengthen relationships, and fuel your drive for success. Let's explore why attitude isn't just important—it's everything.

Turning Challenges into Opportunities

We've all been there. Life throws a curveball, and it feels like the universe is testing your patience. But here's a secret that those with a positive attitude know: challenges aren't the end of the road—they're detours leading to new adventures.

When faced with setbacks, people with a positive mindset don't throw in the towel. Instead, they ask, "What went wrong, and how can I do better next time?" This mindset turns failures into feedback, fostering growth instead of defeat.

Think of it like this: A positive attitude is like having a GPS that recalculates after every wrong turn, guiding you toward success no matter how bumpy the road gets.

The Magic of Relationships

Ever noticed how some people seem to attract others like magnets? They radiate warmth, kindness, and positivity, making those around them feel valued and comfortable. That's the magic of a positive attitude at work.

When you have a positive outlook, you communicate better, listen more intently, and show empathy. You're not just focused on what you can gain from others but on what you can give. This generosity strengthens bonds, whether with family, friends, or coworkers.

Picture this: You're part of a team project. One member constantly complains and highlights problems, while another focuses on solutions and encourages the group. Who would you rather work with? Exactly! A positive attitude doesn't just make life easier for you—it lifts others up, too.

Fueling Your Motivation and Drive

What gets you out of bed on those days when you'd rather hit snooze indefinitely? For those with a positive attitude, it's their belief in possibilities. They don't see obstacles as roadblocks but as puzzles are waiting to be solved.

Think of attitude as the spark that ignites motivation. When you believe your efforts matter, you stay persistent and focused, even when the going gets tough. A positive attitude drives you forward, reminding you that each step, no matter how small, brings you closer to your goals.

Take athletes, for example. They don't win because they avoid failure— they win because they don't let failure stop them. They keep showing up, learning, and improving. That's the power of positivity—it fuels perseverance.

Mental and Emotional Resilience

Life is unpredictable, and maintaining a positive attitude doesn't mean pretending everything's perfect. It means choosing how you respond, even when things aren't going your way.

A positive mindset acts as emotional armor. Stressful day at work? Instead of spiraling into frustration, remind yourself, "This is temporary. I can handle it." Got bad news? Instead of feeling overwhelmed, focus on what you can control and seek solutions.

This shift in perspective does wonders for your mental health. Studies show that people who practice positivity have lower levels of stress, anxiety, and depression. It's not that they live in a bubble of rainbows and unicorns—they simply focus on what they can change rather than what they can't.

Attitude and Your Physical Health

Here's something surprising: your attitude directly impacts your health. Ever heard of the placebo effect? It's the phenomenon where people heal faster or feel better simply because they believe they will. That's the mind-body connection in action.

Positive thinkers tend to have lower blood pressure, stronger immune systems, and quicker recovery from illnesses. Why? Because a positive attitude reduces stress—a major culprit behind many health issues. When you're less stressed, your body functions better. It's as if positivity is your body's built-in health insurance.

And here's the bonus: People with positive attitudes often make healthier choices. They exercise, eat well, and sleep better because they value their well-being. It's a win-win for both mind and body.

Confidence Booster

Let's talk confidence. You know that feeling when you're unstoppable, like you could conquer the world? A positive attitude helps you get there.

When you believe in yourself and maintain an optimistic outlook, you're more likely to step outside your comfort zone. Whether it's asking for a promotion, starting a new business, or learning a new skill, a positive attitude gives you the courage to take risks and grow.

Confidence isn't about never failing—it's about knowing you can bounce back. People with positive attitudes don't shy away from challenges because they believe in their ability to overcome them. That kind of self-assurance leads to personal growth and success.

Creating Your Own Luck

Ever wondered why some people seem to "get lucky" all the time? It's not luck—it's their attitude. A positive outlook makes you more open to opportunities, connections, and ideas that others might overlook.

When you approach life with optimism, you're naturally more curious and proactive. Instead of waiting for good things to happen, you go out and make them happen. You take calculated risks, meet new people, and pursue your goals with enthusiasm. This opens doors to opportunities that wouldn't exist if you were focused on what could go wrong.

Positivity isn't just a mindset—it's a magnet for success.

Conclusion: The Attitude Advantage

At the end of the day, life is full of twists and turns. You can't always control what happens, but you can absolutely control how you respond. That's where the power of a positive attitude comes in. It shapes your perception of challenges, builds meaningful relationships, fuels your motivation, and even boosts your health.

So, if you want to live a more fulfilling, successful, and joyful life, the secret is simple: start with your attitude. Choose to see the world through the lens of possibility, and watch how your experiences transform for the better.

After all, attitude isn't just everything—it's the key to unlocking your best life.

At Rajchandra University campus at Dharampur,
Gujarat state

CHAPTER 2

Understanding Attitude

Ever had one of those days where nothing seems to go right? You spill coffee on yourself, miss the bus, and then get chewed out by your boss. One person might see it as a sign that the universe is out to get them. But someone else might shrug, laugh it off, and think, "Well, it can only get better from here."

What's the difference between these two? You guessed it: attitude.

So, what's yours doing for you? Is it helping you move forward or keeping you stuck? Let's dive in and find out how a simple shift in attitude can totally transform your life.

***

1.   Your Attitude Is Like a Selfie Filter

We all know those Instagram filters that can make a dull picture look vibrant—or, let's be real, make you look way better than you feel. Well, your attitude is just like that—it's the filter through which you see the world.

Imagine this: Two people are stuck in a traffic jam.

Person A bangs their fists on the steering wheel, complaining about how late they'll be.

Person B cranks up their favorite playlist, calls an old friend, and maybe even appreciates the forced break.

The traffic is the same. The difference? Attitude.

Quick Tip:

Next time life throws you a curveball, ask yourself, "What filter am I using right now?" If it's making everything look worse, it's time to swap it out for something more positive.

***

2. Attitude Is Built, Not Born

Let's clear something up: Attitude isn't something you're stuck with. It's not like your height or eye color—it's more like a playlist. You can change it anytime.

Ever hear someone say, "I'm just not a positive person"? That's like saying, "I can't run a marathon because I've never tried." You can build a stronger, more positive attitude, just like you can train your body. The trick? Repetition and practice. The more you choose positivity, the easier it gets.

Take Viktor Frankl, for example. He survived the Holocaust—one of the darkest periods in human history—yet he believed that the one freedom no one can take from us is the ability to choose our attitude. If he could choose positivity in the worst of situations, what's stopping us?

Actionable Insight:

Start with baby steps. The next time something minor irritates you—like running late or a rude comment—take a breath. Pause. Then choose your attitude. It's like hitting a reset button on your day.

***

3. Want a Life Hack? Attitude Is Your Cheat Code

Ever wished life came with cheat codes like in video games? Spoiler: It kinda does. And that cheat code is a positive attitude.

No, it won't make your problems disappear, but it will change how you deal with them. Think about a challenge you've faced. Did you spiral into frustration, or did you channel that energy into finding a solution? A positive attitude unlocks creativity, resourcefulness, and resilience—everything you need to face challenges head-on.

Pro Move:

Next time you're facing something tough—whether it's a missed opportunity, a rejection, or just a bad day—flip your attitude. Instead of asking, "Why is this happening to me?" ask, "How can this help me grow?" You'll be surprised by the shift in your energy.

***

4. Attitude Is a Vibe—And You're Spreading It

You know that person who walks into a room and instantly lifts the mood? It's not magic—it's attitude.

Whether you realize it or not, your attitude affects everyone around you. It's like a vibe you're constantly broadcasting.

Picture this: You're at a party.

Someone is complaining non-stop about work, the weather, life in general. Suddenly, the fun vibe? Gone.

Someone else walks in, full of positive energy, cracking jokes, and spreading good vibes. Instant mood boost.

That's the power of attitude—it's contagious.

Challenge:

Pay attention to your vibe. What kind of energy are you bringing to the table? If you're in a funk, shake it off. Move, blast some upbeat music, or talk to someone who lifts you up. Your energy has a ripple effect, so make sure you're spreading the good kind.

***

5. Negativity Is a Trap—Don't Fall In

Negativity is sneaky. It starts small—maybe a missed deadline or an annoying comment—and before you know it, you're in a full-blown bad mood.

Here's the thing: Negativity is a trap. The more you feed it, the deeper you sink. And it affects everything—your mood, health, and relationships.

Ever noticed how one little thing can ruin your whole day if you let it? It's like a snowball rolling downhill, gathering speed and growing bigger. Stop it before it gets out of control.

Pro Tip:

When you feel negativity creeping in, hit pause. Take a deep breath, step away, and change your focus. Sometimes, just shifting your attention is enough to stop the downward spiral.

***

6. Shift Happens—Make the Change

Alright, so what if you're stuck in a negative attitude? How do you get out of it? Good news: Changing your attitude is easier than you think.

Three Simple Steps to Shift Your Attitude:

1. Practice gratitude. Sounds simple, but it works. Every day, write down three things you're thankful for. It trains your brain to focus on the positives.

2. Surround yourself with positive influences. People, books, podcasts— your environment shapes your mindset.

3. Reframe your thinking. When something goes wrong, instead of thinking, "Why does this always happen to me?" ask, "What can I learn from this?"

Try This:

The next time something goes sideways, challenge yourself to find the silver lining—even if it's tiny. Over time, this habit will help you build a more positive mindset.

***

7. The Eagle Story: Are You Living Like a Chicken?

Here's a story to think about:

A farmer finds an eagle's egg and, not knowing what to do with it, places it in a nest with his chickens. When the egg hatches, the baby eagle grows up surrounded by chickens. It eats like them, walks like them, and flies only as high as the other chickens can.

One day, the young eagle looks up and sees a majestic bird soaring high in the sky.

"Who is that?" it asks the chickens.

"That's an eagle," they reply. "But you're a chicken. You'll never fly that high."

And just like that, the eagle accepts its fate. It lives and dies like a chicken, never realizing its true potential.

The Moral?

Many of us are like that eagle. We're surrounded by mediocrity and let it convince us that we can't achieve greatness. But here's the truth:

You're an eagle, not a chicken. It's time to soar.

Bottom Line:

Your attitude determines whether you live like a chicken or soar like an eagle. The choice is yours.

Being Interviewed at The International University, Paris. The Palms , Dubai

CHAPTER 3

The Power of Positivity: "Your Attitude Today Shapes Your Success Tomorrow"

Let's kick things off with a quick activity. Grab a piece of paper and a pen, and set a timer for five minutes. In that time, write down three things you're thankful for right now. It could be as simple as your cozy bed or a delicious meal you had. Got it? Great! Now, how do you feel after doing this? A little lighter? Maybe a bit more peaceful? That's the magic of positivity.

This simple exercise taps into the power of gratitude, one of the cornerstones of a positive mindset. But there's so much more to positivity than just feeling good. Ever wondered why some people navigate life's toughest challenges with a smile while others crumble under pressure? It's not luck or some special gift—they've learned to harness the power of positivity. And here's the best part: you can, too.

So, how exactly does a positive mindset influence your brain and emotions? More importantly, how can you practice positivity daily to change your outlook on life? Let's dive into the fascinating science behind positivity and uncover how a few small daily actions can make a world of difference.

The Psychological Benefits of a Positive Mindset

Think of your brain as a muscle. Just like your biceps or abs, it can be trained and strengthened. And guess what positivity does? It flexes your brain in ways that enhance both your emotional and psychological well-being.

1. Positivity Broadens Your Perspective

Psychologist Barbara Fredrickson's Broaden and Build Theory reveals something powerful: when we experience positive emotions, our brains expand their capacity to see more, think creatively, and consider a broader range of possibilities. In contrast, negative emotions narrow our focus, making us dwell on problems and limiting our ability to think clearly or act effectively.

For instance, when you're anxious, it's like having tunnel vision—your brain zeroes in on threats, making it hard to think about anything else. But with positivity, your brain opens up like a panoramic view, allowing you to see not just the obstacles but also the potential solutions. This broader perspective is crucial for facing challenges with a mindset of growth and opportunity.

2. Positivity Rewires Your Brain

Here's the most mind-blowing part: positivity can literally change your brain. According to the principles of neuroplasticity, your brain is constantly evolving based on your experiences and thoughts. When you practice positive thinking, you reinforce neural pathways associated with joy, hope, and optimism. Over time, these pathways become stronger, making it easier for your brain to default to positive thoughts.

In contrast, a negative mindset strengthens the neural pathways linked to stress, anxiety, and despair. In other words, the more you practice negativity, the better your brain becomes at being pessimistic. But the good news? With consistent practice, you can retrain your brain to focus on positivity, ultimately improving your emotional resilience and well-being.

3. Positivity Boosts Emotional Resilience and Reduces Stress

Positivity doesn't mean life becomes a walk in the park. What it does mean, however, is that you develop the resilience to handle stress more effectively. Studies show that people with a positive mindset experience lower levels of cortisol—the stress hormone—and have a greater ability to bounce back after setbacks.

Instead of seeing difficulties as overwhelming, a positive person views them as challenges that can be overcome. This mindset doesn't just protect you emotionally—it benefits you physically, too. Lower stress levels are linked to better heart health, a stronger immune system, and a longer lifespan.

The Impact of Positivity on the Brain and Emotions

Let's take a closer look at how positivity physically and chemically affects the brain and emotions.

1. Dopamine and Serotonin—The "Feel-Good" Chemicals

When you maintain a positive mindset, your brain releases chemicals like dopamine and serotonin—the body's natural feel-good chemicals. These neurotransmitters are responsible for making you feel happy, calm, and fulfilled. When dopamine and serotonin levels are high, your mood improves, and you're more likely to experience a sense of well-being.

Not only do these chemicals elevate your mood, but they also enhance cognitive functions like memory and focus, allowing you to think more clearly and make better decisions.

2. Reduced Amygdala Activity

The amygdala is the part of your brain responsible for the fight-or-flight response. When you're constantly stressed or negative, your amygdala becomes overactive, making you react impulsively to threats—real or imagined.

Positive thinking, however, reduces activity in the amygdala, keeping you calm and composed even in stressful situations. When you cultivate positivity, you're less likely to overreact to problems and more likely to respond thoughtfully and with control.

3. Strengthens the Prefrontal Cortex

The prefrontal cortex is the part of the brain responsible for rational thinking, decision-making, and problem-solving. When you practice positivity, the prefrontal cortex becomes more active, improving your ability to think critically and creatively. This means you're not just happier but also better equipped to tackle challenges head-on.

Daily Practices to Cultivate Positivity

Building a positive mindset isn't about flipping a switch—it's about incorporating small, consistent practices into your daily life. Here are some practical activities you can start today to cultivate positivity:

1. Gratitude Journaling

Every morning or before bed, write down three things you're grateful for. They can be as simple as enjoying a cup of coffee or as significant as spending time with loved ones. This shifts your focus from what's lacking to what's abundant in your life, rewiring your brain to focus on the positive.

2. Positive Affirmations

Start your day by repeating positive affirmations. Whether it's "I am capable of overcoming any challenge" or "I attract positivity into my life," these affirmations can help reframe your mindset. Over time, they'll become ingrained in your subconscious, influencing your thoughts and actions in a positive direction.

3. Random Acts of Kindness

One of the simplest ways to boost positivity is by spreading it to others. Perform small acts of kindness, like sending a kind text, complimenting someone, or helping a coworker. Acts of kindness release oxytocin—the "love hormone"—which enhances your mood and strengthens your connection to others.

4. Mindfulness Meditation

Take five minutes each day to focus on your breath and clear your mind. Mindfulness meditation reduces stress and increases awareness, helping you stay present and grounded. It's a great way to calm your brain and reset your attitude, especially during stressful times.

5. Reframe Negative Thoughts

Whenever you catch yourself in a negative thought spiral, pause and reframe. Instead of thinking, "I'll never get through this," try, "This is tough, but I'm capable of finding a solution." Shifting your inner dialogue from negative to positive helps retrain your brain to respond more optimistically to challenges.

Final Thoughts: The Ripple Effect of Positivity

Positivity isn't just about feeling good in the moment—it's about building a mindset that enhances every aspect of your life. By understanding the science of positivity and incorporating small daily practices, you can rewire your brain, boost your emotional resilience, and navigate life's ups and downs with greater ease and confidence.

Positivity isn't a destination—it's a journey, and every small step you take leads to a more fulfilling, joyful life. So, start today. Make a conscious decision to think positively, and watch as it transforms not just your brain but your entire world.

Doctorate Award given by me to Chairman Dr. Joseph William of REEBOK, UK

CHAPTER 4

Overcoming Negative Thoughts: Your Mind's Ultimate Power Move

Ever had one of those days where it feels like everything's going wrong? You spill your coffee, miss the bus, and then—of course—you get that email that makes your stomach drop. Before you know it, one negative thought snowballs into another, and suddenly, it's not just a bad day; it feels like a bad life. Sound familiar?

If you've ever been caught in a whirlwind of negative thoughts, you're not alone. The truth is, our brains are wired to pay more attention to the bad stuff than the good. It's a survival mechanism from way back in the caveman days when noticing danger was the difference between life and death. The problem? These days, it's not saber-toothed tigers we're running from—it's our own minds.

So how do you stop the cycle of negative thinking before it spirals out of control? How do you recognize when those thoughts are taking over, and more importantly, how do you challenge them? In this chapter, we're going to dive deep into recognizing negative patterns and explore practical techniques to reframe and overcome negativity.

Ready to master your mind? Let's go.

***

Recognizing Negative Thought Patterns: The Sneaky Culprits

The first step to overcoming negative thoughts is recognizing when they're happening. Sounds simple, right? But negative thoughts can be sneaky. They show up disguised as reality, and before you know it, you're down the rabbit hole of self-doubt, anxiety, and stress.

1. The All-or-Nothing Trap

One of the most common negative thought patterns is the all-or-nothing mindset. You know the one: "If I don't succeed at this, I'm a total failure." It's the kind of thinking that leaves no room for middle ground. If something doesn't go perfectly, you convince yourself it's a disaster.

Sound familiar? This pattern can be destructive because it doesn't allow for mistakes, learning, or growth. It makes you believe that anything less than 100% success equals total failure. Spoiler alert: it doesn't.

2. Catastrophizing / Over-Exaggeration

Catastrophizing—the art of turning a molehill into a mountain. This happens when your brain fast-forwards to the worst possible scenario, even if it's wildly unlikely. You think, "I made a mistake at work; now I'm definitely going to get fired, lose my home, and live under a bridge." Pretty dramatic, right?

Our brains love to jump to the worst-case scenario, but more often than not, reality is much less extreme than our thoughts would have us believe.

3. Mental Filtering

Ever had a day where 99 things go right, but you only focus on the one thing that went wrong? That's mental filtering. It's when your brain becomes obsessed with the negative, filtering out anything positive. Even if someone gives you ten compliments and one critique, you'll fixate on that critique like it's the only thing that matters.

Negative filters act like blinders, stopping us from seeing the full picture and making life seem way harder than it actually is.

4. The Blame Game

Negative thoughts often thrive on blame—whether you're blaming yourself for things beyond your control or pointing fingers at others for your frustrations. "If only I were smarter, this wouldn't have happened," or "They always mess things up for me."

This pattern takes away your power to change your situation, keeping you stuck in negativity.

✳✳✳

Reframing and Challenging Negativity: Flip the Script

Now that we've identified the usual suspects of negative thinking, let's get to the good stuff: how to reframe and challenge those thoughts so they don't run your life.

1. Name That Thought

When you catch yourself spiraling into negative thinking, the first step is to acknowledge it. Don't ignore it or push it down—that just gives it more power. Instead, name it. Say to yourself, "I'm catastrophizing right now."

Naming the thought takes away some of its control. It's like shining a light on a monster under the bed—suddenly, it's not so scary anymore.

2. Ask: Is This Thought True?

Here's where you become a detective. When a negative thought pops up, ask yourself, "Is this thought 100% true? Can I absolutely know for sure that it's going to happen?"

Chances are, the answer is no. For example, if you're thinking, "I'm definitely going to fail this project, and everyone will think I'm incompetent," ask yourself, "Really? Is that true? Have I never succeeded at anything before?"

When you start questioning your thoughts, you'll often find that they're built on assumptions and worst-case scenarios, not facts.

3. Reframe the Situation

Once you've challenged the truth of your thought, it's time to reframe it. Instead of thinking, "I'll never be able to do this," try, "This is going to be tough, but I've overcome challenges before, and I'll learn something from this."

Reframing doesn't mean ignoring the problem or pretending it doesn't exist—it just means changing your perspective so that the situation feels more manageable and less overwhelming.

4. Practice Self-Compassion

One of the biggest drivers of negative thinking is a lack of self-compassion. When things go wrong, it's easy to be hard on yourself and expect perfection. But here's the deal: you're human. Perfection doesn't exist.

Instead of beating yourself up, talk to yourself the way you would talk to a friend. If a friend made a mistake, would you say, "Wow, you really messed up, and now your life is ruined"? Of course not. You'd probably say, "It's okay, everyone makes mistakes. You'll figure it out."

Give yourself the same grace and kindness. The more you practice self-compassion, the easier it becomes to break the cycle of negativity.

***

Daily Techniques to Tame Negative Thoughts

Overcoming negative thinking isn't a one-time fix—it's a practice. The good news? A few small daily habits can make a huge difference.

1. Gratitude Practice

Start and end your day by writing down three things you're grateful for. This shifts your focus away from the negative and helps you notice the good things in your life, no matter how small. Gratitude rewires your brain to look for positives, making it harder for negativity to take over.

2. Mindful Breathing

When negative thoughts start to creep in, try some mindful breathing. Focus on your breath—slowly inhaling for four counts, holding for four counts, and exhaling for four counts. This simple practice helps calm your mind and keeps you grounded in the present moment, preventing your thoughts from spiraling out of control.

3. Affirmations

Incorporate positive affirmations into your daily routine. When you wake up, look in the mirror and say, "I am capable of handling anything that comes my way," or "I am worthy of success and happiness." Affirmations might feel cheesy at first, but they help counteract negative self-talk and build a stronger, more positive mindset.

4. Cognitive Restructuring

Cognitive restructuring is a fancy way of saying challenge your thoughts. Whenever a negative thought pops up, break it down. Is it rational? Is it based on facts or fears? By analyzing your thoughts, you can replace irrational negativity with more balanced, realistic thinking.

✳✳✳

The Bottom Line: You're in Control

Overcoming negative thoughts doesn't happen overnight. But here's the thing—you can do it. You're not a prisoner of your mind. By recognizing negative patterns, challenging those thoughts, and practicing small daily techniques, you can flip the script on negativity.

Thoughts don't define you, and they don't control you—unless you let them.

So, next time negativity starts creeping in, pause. Recognize it. Challenge it. And then? Reframe it.

You've got this.

CHAPTER 5

Unlocking Positivity: The Power of Gratitude and Affirmations

Activity: The "Gratitude Treasure Hunt"

Let's start this chapter with something fun and engaging. Think of this as a mini treasure hunt in your daily life. Here's your challenge: as you go about your day, actively look for three things that bring a smile to your face or make you feel good. The catch? These can't be big, obvious things like winning the lottery or getting a job promotion. Instead, they should be small, everyday "treasures" that you often overlook.

It could be the sound of birds chirping outside your window, the warmth of your coffee cup in your hands, or the laughter of a loved one. Once you've found your three treasures, take a moment to savor them—really feel the appreciation for these simple moments. That's it! You've just completed your first "Gratitude Treasure Hunt."

You might be surprised at how powerful this small exercise can be. When you actively search for the good, even in the mundane, you train your mind to focus on the positive aspects of life.

***

Why Gratitude Matters

You may be wondering, "Why does gratitude even matter?" Think of gratitude as a shift in perspective. We all go through life juggling good days and bad days. When things get tough, it's easy to dwell on the problems—work deadlines, piling bills, or a recent argument with a loved one.

But here's the thing: no matter how bad a day might seem, there are always little pockets of joy waiting to be noticed. Gratitude helps us find and focus on those moments. It doesn't make problems disappear, but it changes how we experience them. Instead of seeing life as a constant struggle, gratitude allows us to appreciate what we already have, making the journey feel lighter and brighter.

***

The Science Behind Gratitude

Gratitude isn't just a feel-good concept thrown around in self-help books—it's backed by science. Research shows that people who practice gratitude consistently have better mental and emotional well-being. Here's why:

1. It Rewires Your Brain – Our brains are naturally inclined to focus on negativity (a survival mechanism from our ancestors who had to be on alert for danger). Practicing gratitude retrains your brain to notice the positive more often, reducing stress and increasing happiness.

2. It Reduces Anxiety and Stress – Focusing on what's going well in your life shifts your attention away from stressors. This doesn't mean ignoring problems; rather, it helps you develop a healthier perspective.

3. It Builds Resilience – Life will always throw challenges your way, but when you cultivate gratitude, you strengthen your emotional resilience. You'll find it easier to bounce back from setbacks because you've trained yourself to see the good even in difficult times.

***

Daily Gratitude Practices

How do you make gratitude a part of your daily routine? Here are a few simple yet powerful ways to get started:

1. The One-Minute Gratitude Pause – At any point in your day, take just one minute to pause and think about something you're grateful for. It could be your lunch, the sunny weather, or a supportive colleague. This quick exercise helps refocus your mind.

2. Gratitude Journaling – At the end of each day, jot down three things you're thankful for. They don't have to be major events—just small moments that made you smile or feel content.

3. Gratitude Conversations – The next time you're with a friend or family member, share something you're grateful for. Even a simple mention of something positive can uplift both you and the person you're talking to.

***

The Power of Positive Affirmations

Now, let's talk about another tool for shifting your mindset: positive affirmations.

We all have that inner voice that talks to us throughout the day. Sometimes, it's helpful, but often, it's a critic. It might tell you things like, "I'm not good enough," "I always mess up," or "I'll never be successful." These negative thoughts might feel true, but they're often just stories we've repeated for so long that we believe them.

Positive affirmations help rewrite those stories. They are simple, positive statements that challenge your inner critic and remind you of your potential. Think of affirmations as planting seeds of confidence and positivity in your mind. With regular practice, these seeds grow into strong, empowering beliefs.

***

How Affirmations Work

Here's the science behind why affirmations are effective:

1. Changing Negative Beliefs – Many of our negative beliefs come from past experiences or societal pressures. Repeating affirmations regularly helps replace these limiting beliefs with empowering ones.

2. Boosting Confidence – When you tell yourself, "I am capable" or "I am worthy of success," you gradually start to believe it. Over time, this builds confidence and changes how you approach challenges.

3. Creating a Growth Mindset – Affirmations reinforce the idea that you're constantly evolving and improving, rather than being stuck in old habits or mistakes.

***

Creating Your Own Affirmations

To create effective affirmations, follow these simple guidelines:

1. Make It Present – Instead of saying, "I will be confident," say, "I am confident." Speak as if it's already true to train your brain to align with that reality.

2. Keep It Positive – Focus on what you want, not what you don't want. For example, instead of saying, "I don't want to be stressed," say, "I am calm and centered."

3. Be Specific – Tailor your affirmations to your needs. If you're looking to boost self-esteem, say, "I am deserving of love and respect."

✳✳✳

Examples of Powerful Affirmations

"I am capable of achieving my goals."

"I am worthy of happiness and success."

"I attract positive opportunities into my life."

"I handle challenges with grace and strength."

✳✳✳

Making Affirmations a Habit

Affirmations work best when they become a part of your daily routine. Here's how to integrate them into your day:

1. Morning Routine – Start your day by saying your affirmations out loud, preferably in front of a mirror. This boosts confidence and sets a positive tone for the day.

2. Sticky Note Reminders – Write your affirmations on sticky notes and place them where you'll see them often—on your bathroom mirror, fridge, or desk.

3. Affirmations on the Go – Record yourself saying affirmations and listen to them during your commute, workout, or while doing household chores. Repeating them regularly reinforces the message.

Gratitude and Affirmations: A Winning Combination

Gratitude and affirmations are a powerful duo. Gratitude keeps you grounded in the present and helps you appreciate what you already have, while affirmations push you toward the future you want to create.

Together, they form a strong foundation for cultivating a positive attitude. When combined, you celebrate the good in your life while empowering yourself to grow and achieve even more.

Conclusion: Your Path to a Positive Mindset

You've now learned two powerful tools for shifting your mindset: gratitude and positive affirmations. The key to success lies in consistency. Start small—whether it's your daily "Gratitude Treasure Hunt" or repeating a few affirmations in the morning. Over time, these practices will reshape how you see the world and yourself.

Remember, it's not about ignoring life's challenges—it's about choosing to focus on the good and believing in your ability to shape your future. Your journey to a positive attitude has already begun. Keep going—you're on the right path!

CHAPTER 6

Resilience and Positivity in Tough Times

Challenging situations never knock on our doors to seek permission before entering our lives.

Scratching your head? Let me explain with a small scenario:

"Sarah, it's going to be okay," her mind repeated, but her heart felt like it was in free fall. She gripped the phone tighter, her knuckles turning white as the words sank in. Her husband was in critical condition after a severe accident. She had two small kids at home, a demanding job, and now this. Life had taken an unexpected turn, and it felt like the ground beneath her had just crumbled.

As she stared out of the hospital window later that night, Sarah realized something important: while she couldn't control what had happened to her husband, she could control one thing—how she responded to it. "I've got this," she told herself, almost in defiance of the crushing weight on her shoulders.

Now, don't get me wrong. Sarah wasn't some superhero. She cried. She broke down. But she always found her way back. How? By leaning into resilience and maintaining a positive mindset, even when it felt impossible. And isn't that what we all want to do when life throws us curveballs? Stay positive, keep moving, and find the strength within.

***

What Exactly Is Resilience?

Resilience isn't about being bulletproof. It's about bouncing back, even when life hits hard. Think of it like a rubber band—you can stretch it, twist it, and pull it apart, but somehow, it snaps back into place. That's resilience. It's not about avoiding hardship but facing it head-on and emerging stronger.

And here's the thing—resilience is not some magical trait that only a few people are born with. You, too, can build it, nurture it, and grow it. It's a skill that strengthens over time, just like learning a new instrument or practicing yoga.

***

The Secret Sauce: Positivity

Let's be clear—positivity doesn't mean wearing rose-colored glasses and pretending everything is sunshine and rainbows when it's clearly not. It's about acknowledging the reality of a tough situation but choosing to focus on what you can do, what's still good, and what's possible. It's the belief that better days are ahead, no matter how distant they seem.

When Sarah was juggling hospital visits, work, and home life, she had two choices: dwell on the unfairness of the situation or search for the small moments of hope. Sure, her husband was in critical condition, but he was alive. Yes, her world was upside down, but she had friends stepping in to help with the kids. These were her small sparks of light amidst the chaos.

So, how do we tap into that positivity during tough times?

***

Let's Break It Down: How to Cultivate Resilience and Positivity

Building resilience and staying positive isn't something you master overnight, but with a little daily effort, it can transform how you face challenges. Here's how:

1. Flip the Script

Ever notice how easy it is to focus on what's going wrong? Our brains are wired to spot danger and prepare for the worst. But what if, instead of asking, "Why is this happening to me?", you asked, "What can I learn from this?" This simple shift reframes challenges as opportunities for growth rather than obstacles.

2. Start a Gratitude Ritual

When Sarah's life felt like it was falling apart, she began writing down three things she was grateful for each day. Some days, it was as simple as, "I got five minutes of peace with my coffee." Other days, it was something more profound, like, "My husband smiled today." Focusing on the good doesn't erase the bad, but it helps balance negativity and makes room for positivity.

3. Set Micro-Goals

When life is overwhelming, the thought of tackling a huge problem can feel impossible. Break it down into micro-goals—small, achievable steps that keep you moving forward. Sarah didn't plan her entire week at once. She started with, "Today, I'll call the doctor and make sure the kids get to school." That's it. One step forward is progress, and progress fuels positivity.

4. Lean on Your Tribe

Resilient people know they can't do it alone. Sarah reached out to her family and friends for support—whether it was a meal, a kind word, or just someone to sit with her at the hospital. Asking for help isn't a sign of weakness; it's a strength. Sometimes, it's the only way to refill your cup when it's running dry.

5. Practice Mindfulness

Mindfulness isn't about maintaining Zen-like calm 24/7. It's about being present in the moment—whether it's a good one or a tough one. During her hardest moments, Sarah would take five minutes to just breathe. No phone, no distractions. Just her and her breath. This simple act of grounding herself helped her regain focus and perspective when everything felt like too much.

***

Positivity as a Habit, Not a Quick Fix

Here's the kicker: positivity is a habit, not a one-time solution. It's something you need to work on continuously, especially during difficult times. The more you practice it, the more naturally it will come to you when life throws its inevitable challenges your way.

***

Wrapping It Up: The Power of Positivity in Action

Let's revisit Sarah's story. Her husband eventually recovered, but more importantly, so did she. And the person she became after the ordeal wasn't the same as the one before. Sarah was stronger, more resilient, and more grateful for life's small wins.

Resilience and positivity didn't just get her through the tough times—they transformed her.

Now, imagine you are in the middle of a tough situation—whether it's work stress, relationship struggles, or personal loss. How would it feel to know that no matter what life throws at you, you have the tools to face it head-on with resilience and positivity? Pretty empowering, right?

***

Your Turn: Building Your Resilience Toolbox

Here's an activity to get you started. Think of it as your personal Resilience Booster.

Step 1: Get a notebook or open a note on your phone.

Step 2: Write down three challenges you're currently facing.

Step 3: For each challenge, answer these three questions:

1. What can I learn from this?

2. What is one small thing I can do today to improve the situation?

3. What is something positive in my life that I can focus on to balance this challenge?

Do this every day for a week. You'll start to notice that challenges feel less overwhelming when you shift your focus to action and gratitude.

Remember, resilience isn't about avoiding storms—it's about learning to dance in the rain.

So, are you ready to start your dance?

@ Press conference for Award Ceremony

CHAPTER 7

Mindfulness and Physical Well-being

"The body benefits from movement, and the mind benefits from stillness."

— Sakyong Mipham

Let's Begin with a Quick Activity

Before diving into the topic, take a moment to try this simple exercise with me. Find a comfortable place to sit, close your eyes, and take three deep breaths—slowly in through your nose and out through your mouth. As you inhale, feel the air filling your lungs and expanding your chest. As you exhale, let go of any tension in your body. Now, gently bring your attention to how your body feels. Maybe you notice the pressure of the chair beneath you or the rise and fall of your breath.

That's mindfulness in action—being fully present in your body, even for just a few moments.

Doesn't that feel grounding? This small shift in attention is the first step toward understanding the connection between mindfulness and physical well-being.

What Exactly Is Mindfulness?

Picture this: You're in the middle of a busy day, your phone is buzzing, your mind is already racing through tomorrow's to-do list, and suddenly you realize—you can't even remember what you had for lunch. Ever feel like you're on autopilot, just moving through the motions of life without really being there? That's the opposite of mindfulness.

Mindfulness is like hitting the "pause" button in the chaos. It's the art of being fully present—of noticing the details of the moment you're in—without letting your mind spin in circles over the past or future. Sounds simple, right? But it's a game-changer.

Instead of drifting through your day, imagine feeling completely connected—to your body, to your breath, to the world around you. And here's the twist: the benefits aren't just about feeling more centered or calm. The real magic is how this kind of presence can transform your physical well-being. We're talking better sleep, less stress, improved digestion, and even a stronger immune system—all from simply tuning into the here and now.

So, when we explore the relationship between mindfulness and physical well-being, we're diving into how living more intentionally—more aware—can unlock some pretty amazing health benefits. And honestly, who wouldn't want that?

How Mindfulness Impacts the Body

Mindfulness isn't just about feeling calm or peaceful; it has real, tangible effects on the body. Studies show that mindfulness practices like meditation, breathing exercises, and mindful movement (such as yoga) lead to measurable improvements in physical health. Let's break it down:

1. Reducing Stress and Its Physical Effects

We've all heard that stress is a "silent killer," but have you ever stopped to consider why? Chronic stress floods the body with cortisol, a hormone meant to help us in emergencies. However, when cortisol levels remain elevated due to ongoing stress, it wreaks havoc on the body. It raises blood pressure, suppresses the immune system, and even contributes to weight gain.

Mindfulness acts as a buffer against this stress response. When you're mindful, you step out of the endless loop of worry, fear, and tension, giving your body a chance to relax and heal. By regularly practicing mindfulness, you essentially train your body to react less intensely to stress, keeping cortisol levels in check and helping your body stay balanced.

2. Boosting Immune Function

Ever noticed how you're more likely to catch a cold or feel run-down when you're stressed? That's no coincidence. Mindfulness strengthens the immune system by reducing inflammation in the body. Research has shown that people who practice mindfulness regularly have higher levels of antibodies, which help fight off infections and illnesses.

It's like giving your immune system a VIP pass to stay alert and effective, even in the face of everyday stressors.

3. Improving Sleep Quality

If you've ever tossed and turned, lying awake for hours, you know how elusive sleep can be when your mind is racing. Mindfulness quiets the chatter in your head, making it easier to wind down and fall asleep. It also promotes deeper, more restful sleep, which is essential for the body's repair and regeneration processes. Without adequate sleep, the body can't properly heal, leading to a weakened immune system, chronic fatigue, and even weight gain.

4. Enhancing Digestion

Our minds and bodies are more connected than we often realize. Have you ever eaten a meal while distracted, only to realize afterward that you didn't even taste the food? Or worse, have you felt bloated or uncomfortable after eating too quickly?

Mindful eating is one of the most powerful ways mindfulness can improve physical well-being. When you pay attention to what you're eating—savoring each bite, noticing how your body feels as you chew—you actually aid your digestive system. This reduces overeating and helps your body process food more efficiently.

Mindfulness in Everyday Life

Okay, so mindfulness clearly has some serious benefits for the body. But how do we actually practice mindfulness in our daily lives? Many people think mindfulness is something you can only do while sitting cross-legged on a meditation cushion, but that's not true. Mindfulness can be woven into everyday activities like eating, walking, or even brushing your teeth. The key is to slow down and focus on the experience as it's happening.

1. Mindful Breathing

This is perhaps the simplest and most accessible form of mindfulness. Anytime you feel stressed, anxious, or disconnected, take a few slow, deep breaths. Inhale deeply through your nose, hold for a second, and exhale through your mouth. Focus on the sensation of your breath entering and leaving your body. In just a few minutes, you'll likely notice a drop in tension and an increase in calm.

2. Mindful Walking

Next time you go for a walk, leave your phone at home and focus on each step. Feel the ground beneath your feet, notice the air on your skin, and observe the sounds around you. This not only keeps you grounded in the present but also encourages gentle movement, which is great for circulation and overall physical well-being.

3. Mindful Eating

At your next meal, try to eat without any distractions—no TV, no phone, just you and your food. Chew slowly and notice the flavors, textures, and smells of each bite. Listen to your body's cues for hunger and fullness. You'll find you enjoy your food more and feel more satisfied without overeating or feeling sluggish afterward.

4. Body Scanning

Body scanning is a powerful mindfulness technique that helps you reconnect with your physical self. Starting from your toes, slowly work your way up your body, paying attention to how each part feels. Is there tension in your shoulders? A dull ache in your back? The more you practice body scanning, the more attuned you become to the subtle signals your body sends—signals that are easy to miss when we're distracted by daily life.

Your Next Step: A 5-Minute Mindfulness Practice

Here's an activity you can start right now to bring mindfulness into your daily routine:

1. Set a Timer for 5 Minutes

Find a quiet spot, sit comfortably, and close your eyes.

2. Focus on Your Breath

Inhale deeply through your nose, feeling the air fill your lungs. Exhale slowly through your mouth. Focus all your attention on your breath.

3. Notice Your Body

As you breathe, gently scan your body from head to toe. Notice any tension or tightness, and with each exhale, imagine releasing it.

4. Be Present

If your mind starts to wander (which it will), gently bring it back to your breath and your body.

That's it! Simple, right? But don't underestimate its power. With just five minutes a day, you'll start to see improvements in your physical well-being— more energy, better sleep, reduced stress, and an overall sense of balance.

In a world that moves fast, mindfulness invites us to slow down, breathe, and truly connect with our bodies. It's not just a practice; it's a way of living that can transform your health from the inside out.

With Tata Group's Chairman Shri Ratan Tata, India

CHAPTER 8

A Twist of Words: How Positive Communication Transformed a Workplace

Once upon a time, in a bustling office full of bright minds, a problem was brewing. The sales team, led by Sam, was struggling to meet targets, and frustration had seeped into the workplace. Conversations became short and curt, emails turned into blunt orders, and meetings felt tense. The negative energy in the office was palpable—until one day, something changed.

It all started when a new intern, Anya, joined the team. On her first day, she sensed the heavy atmosphere but chose to act differently. When she received her first task, instead of the usual "Got it," she responded with, "Thank you for trusting me with this—I'll do my best!"

Her enthusiasm caught the team by surprise, especially Sam, who was used to hearing only complaints and stress. Inspired by her positivity, others began to follow suit. Little by little, "thanks" and "well done" replaced silence, and soon, even Sam started meetings by recognizing small wins. Within weeks, sales improved, and the entire office vibe shifted for the better.

Applying a Positive Attitude in Your Work

Positive communication is contagious, and its benefits go far beyond just creating a happier environment. It strengthens relationships, boosts productivity, and leads to better results. But maintaining a positive attitude doesn't just happen—it's something you cultivate actively, day by day, thought by thought.

Here's an activity to kick-start that process:

Activity: The Appreciation Ripple

For this exercise, commit to expressing gratitude and encouragement intentionally. Try these steps:

1. Morning Reflection

Start each day by writing down three things you appreciate about your work, colleagues, or environment. Even small things count, like a good cup of coffee or a quick chat with a coworker.

2. Spread the Words

Aim to say or write three specific, positive things to three different people throughout your workday. It could be as simple as thanking someone for their help or complimenting a colleague's hard work.

3. Weekly Check-In

At the end of each week, reflect on how your interactions have changed. Are conversations flowing more easily? Do you feel more connected to others? Take note of any shifts in your own attitude and how positivity is making work more enjoyable.

This simple practice not only spreads positivity to others but also has a boomerang effect, bringing joy back to you. Just like in Sam's team, small changes can create ripples that lead to big waves—waves that carry you toward success!

Receiving CNBC Award at Taj, Mumbai, India

CHAPTER 9

Embracing a Lasting Positive Attitude – Your Final Step Forward

As you reach the final chapter of this journey on building and nurturing a positive attitude, take a moment to recognize how far you've come. Cultivating a genuinely positive outlook isn't a quick sprint but a steady, intentional walk—one that requires resilience, self-awareness, and, most importantly, joy. This chapter isn't about adding more to your plate; it's about preserving, deepening, and fully living the positivity you've cultivated.

Embracing Growth as a Lifelong Journey

Positivity isn't a fixed destination—it's a lifelong adventure. A positive attitude is like a garden; it requires regular care to stay vibrant. With every challenge, milestone, or setback, remind yourself that maintaining positivity means seeing each experience as an opportunity for growth. Ask yourself: How can this situation help me grow? How can I respond with grace?

Every experience—whether joyful or difficult—is a step forward. A sustained positive outlook allows you to adapt and evolve rather than remain stuck in a single mindset. Instead of seeing change as a threat, view it as a doorway to new opportunities.

***

Nurturing Self-Belief

One of the cornerstones of a lasting positive attitude is unwavering self-belief. Along this journey, you've likely encountered moments of doubt—some of which may have felt overwhelming. But this is exactly when your commitment to self-belief matters most.

A positive attitude is also a belief in your ability to adapt, learn, and thrive. Keep an inner dialogue that empowers you. Regularly affirm your strengths and reflect on past achievements, no matter how small. By consistently nurturing self-belief, you build a strong foundation that will carry you through both challenges and triumphs.

***

Practicing Gratitude Daily

Gratitude is one of the most powerful forces in sustaining a positive attitude. Consider ending each day with a brief moment of gratitude, reflecting on something that brought you joy or a lesson you learned. It doesn't have to be grand—a stranger's smile, a warm meal, or a quiet moment of solitude can be enough.

By consistently recognizing and appreciating the good in your life, you invite more of it. Gratitude shifts your mindset, helping you focus on what's right rather than fixating on what's wrong.

***

Building Positive Habits for Consistency

Sustaining positivity isn't about a single leap—it's about small, steady habits that reinforce your mindset over time. Practices like mindfulness, exercise, and journaling help maintain the positive changes you've made.

Identify simple daily habits that uplift you, and commit to them. Take five minutes each morning to visualize a positive day ahead or practice deep breathing when stressed. Over time, these habits will shape your reactions, making positivity a natural response rather than a forced effort.

***

Embracing a Community of Positivity

Positivity flourishes in the company of those who share a similar outlook. Surround yourself with people who encourage, inspire, and uplift you.

Whether in person or online, connect with communities that promote growth, optimism, and encouragement.

A positive attitude isn't just about how you interact with the world—it's also about the people you allow into your inner circle. The more you engage with individuals who inspire and challenge you, the more naturally positivity will become a part of your life.

***

Accepting Imperfection with Grace

One of the keys to lasting positivity is embracing imperfection—not only in the world around you but also in yourself. Life's journey will include unplanned detours, and not every day will feel like a success. In those moments, remind yourself that it's perfectly okay to feel frustrated, tired, or uncertain.

Positivity isn't about ignoring reality or suppressing emotions—it's about acknowledging them, allowing them to pass, and choosing not to dwell on them. By accepting imperfection, you create a compassionate, flexible approach to sustaining your positive attitude.

***

Living with Purpose and Passion

A positive attitude is most fulfilling when paired with a sense of purpose. As you complete this book, ask yourself: What drives me? What excites me? What fulfills me? Living with purpose—whether it's helping others, creating, or learning—fuels lasting motivation and positivity.

Each day, commit to nurturing your purpose. Let it be the force that strengthens your positive outlook, giving it depth and resilience. When your positivity is rooted in purpose, it becomes more than a mindset—it becomes a way of life.

Conclusion: Moving Forward with an Empowered Attitude

You've journeyed through the highs and lows of developing a positive attitude, building resilience, and finding joy in everyday moments. Remember, sustaining this mindset isn't about achieving perfection—it's about showing up for yourself, honoring your strengths, and being compassionate through your weaknesses.

Take what you've learned in this book and make it your own. You already have everything you need within you to face the world with grace, courage, and joy. Embrace life with an open heart and an empowered attitude, and watch as doors open to endless possibilities.

Here's to your journey ahead—may it be filled with light, growth, and unwavering positivity.

Proofreading & Editing by:

Tulika B. Mukherjee (Proprietor, Katalyka Consultancy Foundation for Education & Empowerment, Gandhinagar, Gujarat)

Gayatri S. Bhattacharya (Proofreader, Katalyka Consultancy Foundation for Education & Empowerment, Gujarat)

Rajvi Desai (Daughter of Dr. Ajay Desai)